Impunity

Impunity

Shelley Stenhouse

NŊY Books™

The New York Quarterly Foundation, Inc.
New York, New York

NYQ Books™ is an imprint of The New York Quarterly Foundation, Inc.

The New York Quarterly Foundation, Inc.
P. O. Box 2015
Old Chelsea Station
New York, NY 10113

www.nyqbooks.org

First Edition

Set in Adobe Garamond Pro

Layout and Design by Raymond P. Hammond

Cover photo from the Shelley Stenhouse archives.

Library of Congress Control Number: 2010907951

ISBN: 978-1-935520-22-1

Impunity

Acknowledgments

Many thanks to the editors of the journals and the anthology in which the following poems have appeared:

"Pants," "Quit It" in *The Antioch Review*; "The Blue Dress" in *Margie*; "AIDS," "Frank," "Mark Roblin," "Victoria's Secrets Are My Sister's Secrets," "You Didn't Last" in *Mudfish*; "Yaddo," "A Lot of Talking in a Lot of Beds," "The Retreat," "Japan Dark," "Snow Day" in *The New York Quarterly*; "John Something" in *Prairie Schooner*; "Mother and Joan in the Diner" in *Quarterly West*; "Pants" in *Samsara Quarterly* (online); "Father With Cow Head," "Impunity," "Russell's Dream" in *Washington Square*.

"Circling" first appeared in *Poetry After 9/11: An Anthology of New York Poets*, edited by Dennis Loy Johnson and Valerie Merians, published by Melville House Press, 2002.

Eighteen poems in this collection first appeared in *PANTS*, winner of the Pavement Saw Press Chapbook Award, 1998-1999 (selected by Ruth Anderson Barnett), and published by Pavement Saw Press in 1999.

I would also like to thank The Corporation of Yaddo, the Writers Room, and The New York Foundation for the Arts; and thanks also to the many friends who have helped birth this book, especially Tony Gloeggler, Judy Rhodes, Libby Schoettle, Caila Rossi, Matthew Gaddis, Tony Hoagland, Douglas Goetsch, Angelo Verga, Miles Stenhouse, Daisygreen Stenhouse, Ted Jonathan, Raymond Hammond and *The New York Quarterly*.

For Daisygreen

Daisy, the day's eye,
green, filled with spring,
Daisygreen, bright field
where daisies grow, your
favorite weather is rain.

IMPUNITY: from A to Z (almost)

AA

Have we always been at war with Eurasia?
I have to re-read 1984. I remember a room
and singing and ripped-off clothes and laundry
hanging in a dirty courtyard. Am I
making this up? Summer is as distant
as an old phone number. It used to live
in my fingers but now I look at my hand
and it ran away and joined the circus.
A fat smile and ripped fishnets. Men
watching, eating peanuts, swilling thin
beer, throwing shells at me and I suck them
for the salt. That would make a good T-shirt
slogan. My old therapist said once good is good
but it's so hard to remember why it matters.
I check my messages like a hand
washing compulsion. Isn't there a pill?
My latest, Lexapro, isn't working.
I say it's a whore who works Lexington
Avenue. If she's inside of me, I'm strong.
All those hours in the blue room
with the ritual of gratitude, the sad
brave hope. Lunch is flat and wide.
I can believe in eyeshadow.
I can believe in coffee.

Adam

Today I fell in love with a violin
teacher. He unlocked a door
at the school, walked through it
with six little girls carrying little violins.
I heard them call him Adam. I saw
his mouth move, through the window—
This is the bow, these are the strings,
sloe-eyed girls staring, *Pull it,*
pull the bow gently across the strings,
hear the sound it makes, feel that, watch
my finger tremble above it, that is music
girls, my finger hovering there.
That's the essence, girls.

Adam, what does essence mean?

Essence, he says, looking out the window,
maybe noticing my hair, turning like leaves,
is that moment before things turn, that moment
when something sings, when the bird
sees something, a cloud moving fast maybe,
lifts his head, and the thought SING
fills not his head but his heart
and goes straight from his heart out his mouth
passing thought altogether.

I want his dark hair on my pillow,
want him in my girl sheets
that make men look sweet.
I am jealous of the thin waist
of his violin, the way she tucks herself
under his chin where I want to be.
I will walk through that door,

interrupt his class, *I'm what the bird sees,*
I'll tell him, *your violin*
before the bow slides across its neck,
wood waiting to sing.

But I turn, shuffle down the hall.
Essence, hear it hiss away
as you say it?

AIDS

I couldn't help thinking about your penis,
that deflated party balloon, that old thin
dachshund hanging behind the dark curtain
of your pants. I knew I should have been thinking
how sad it is I have to lift you into a cab,
wearing a turtleneck in the middle of summer,
your huge voice booming out of a stick figure
from Hangman, with your draft-dodging story,
your dinner theater story, your lecture
on the afterlife. Handing me a copy of your
voice-over tape, small legacy, while I cut up
your food. I'll forget about the money you owe me.
But I thought about your penis, put away in there,
packed away like a used-up catnip toy in a shoe
box, in the small dark room behind your pants,
where the ghosts of all the men and women you have
slept with are mourning, leaning over that long
thing in the coffin, mourning.

Ballad of the Handyman

Each night I dream I'm at his door.
He wears a particle mask, a blue
pocket T-shirt covered with wood dust,
the slow big shoes my cat was always scared of.
It's impossible to tell how he feels, and I don't ask.

The bathroom is built now,
the rest of the apartment is still dark and raw.
He lifts up his mask. We don't talk much.
He shows me his faucet fixtures,
tells where he bought them,
what were the other choices.
This is the cold water, Sweetie. He turns on the tap.
This is the hot. See? You can mix them.
Wanna see the shower? He reaches in,
turns it on, I'm standing in steam
right next to his powerful arm.

We used to take showers together at 3 in the morning
in the old bathroom with the Jesus nightlight.
He never had more than a sliver of soap
and tar shampoo that was thick and brown.
He takes my hand, leads me to his musty bed
behind the canvas tarp. He undresses me
very very slowly for our long silent separate trips
to the places we go when we come together.
For me sometimes it's a London taxi, don't ask me why,
maybe Russell rides a tractor through an Iowa field.

All over the city this morning, handymen in white vans
deliver. They carry bread and beer and ladders,
they weatherproof, sand floors, fix roofs,
they transport furniture, filing cabinets, tools and doors,

they fix pumps, motors, fans, with their hammer-widened
arms, their rough scarred hands. They're invisible
until you love one, then you see them double-
parked on every street, wearing worker caps,
pencils tucked behind their ears.

The Blue Dress

My mother, that last long binge at the Gramercy Park Hotel,
holed up with Dwaynne—
she took me shopping in a ladies' boutique,
drunk, distracted, worried about Dwaynne,
a worthless cracker with a cocaine nail
who'd thrown a beer can at her earlier.
She bought me a blue French dress,
tight in the armpits, a little frumpy,
but the best for sale in that small store
and I had to have something for myself.
I remember how much it cost,
the mean smile, the lecture,
the embarrassment at the counter
when her credit card wouldn't work
because Dwaynne had overrun it,
the way the dress sat folded,
clean and crisp in tissue in the bag,
the suede platform shoes I bought later
to wear with it, the feeling I had
that my arms were too long
but my life might be too short.
The dress was high-waisted, I was high-minded
but also sort of a whore like my mom—
not the kind who did it for a fine French meal,
no—I did it for a look, a touch, a compliment,
a couple of hours spent while I unrolled the thick hairy rug of my life.
Vague dates listened glaze-eyed, smoked, drank, waited
to feel me up under the blue dress my mother bought.

Circling

At night the fighter planes circle
and I look at the yellowed corner of my ceiling
where the dead mosquito hangs
and remember last summer's fear of disease-
bearing bugs, the whoosh of the mosquito trucks,
and my favorite Post headline LET US SPRAY.
Lately I'm afraid of all sounds and the lack of sounds.
News voices, *guarding reactors*—my daughter
hates the news, why is she watching?
And where have the backyard birds gone?
The *yo babay mo-fo boom chicka* Jersey cars
don't blast around my block trying to park.
We'll never go back. It's so strange to be caught
in history, to be making history after just making loads
of unused imaginary money, men in blue jackets shouted,
traded, and it's gone and it's okay but I don't want to die.
I hope God is circling up there with those planes.
Patti was a good person and she died.
God is probably passed out somewhere warm and dark,
still sleeping off his whole world, seven day binge
and it's just us, warring unhinged teenagers
trashing this big beautiful park.

Daguerreotype of Mike

Sometimes I picture you—your threadbare elegance,
the patina of poverty on your crash cut face,
your mouth a soft fancy bow from an era
of tea and country talk, afternoons of polite
shooting in suede shouldered hunting coats,
a Chekhov mouth, incongruously drooling—
a needle dangling from your arm, knotted
necktie maybe or that junkie rubber straining
your veins tight while they wake you
to get you onstage. This scene, burnt spoon,
makes me horny, and the woman who stalked you
across Europe, banging on your various hotel doors
Lee-o-nard Co-hen, Lee-o-nard Co-hen, she didn't
care anymore about the mistake she'd made,
the mixed-up identity, you were Cohen now,
you'd written those songs, it was you
she wanted. That world of blue-red
pick-up sticks, people fixing themselves
until they were ruined, Chelsea Hotel,
curtains drawn, bed and food in the bed
and fucking in the bed and maybe even
pissing the bed—the late the lost, all
the time they have, I envy. Wooster group.
I used to pass that garage and think I'm not
hip enough, ugly enough, thin enough to be
there and I always wonder if you were the one
I saw years ago on the corner of Broadway
and Third, talking to Willem Dafoe, the two
of you an auditorium of cheekbones.
Such a fussbudget now, except for those days
when I called the bed a raft, *we're adrift,*
I said, *there's no way back to land, we're caught
in a storm but we're safe* and we watched
Dick Van Dyke shows, tape after tape.

Disassembly Instructions

Many have unzipped my dress, unhooked my bra,
set free my breasts—you, I want to go farther.
First, undo my tendons like garters, roll down
this skin, help me to step out of it, then tear
my ribs open fast as a bodice, unlatch
the window barred with bone, through it, see a hill
of hidden blood, and in the center of that hill, a tree,
snip its branches like Fagin's gloves—
Reach in, they'll fit your fingers, now grab
the root of my heart, but before you steal
that flower, that jewel, come so close
your breath turns the blue red—
my uncut love has just been cut,
spill it warm all over your hand.

Easter Sunday

A man on a park bench peels a painted egg,
shell as blue as the bright American sky.
He chews it slowly, swallows
the yolk as if he's eating sun.
Each bite makes the day darker.
No salt. No pepper. No plans.

A woman floats by, on the arm
of her boyfriend or husband, his gold-filled
head leaning back in laughter.
If I'd lived at the turn
of the last century,
I might have been
a kept woman, letting her hair down too often.
Someone a painter paints naked, surrounded
by soft cats. Sending scented letters
full of wax seals and curlicues and sad
observations. Sundays, in a straight-
backed chair, I would dream of freedom.

I grew up with money and a pool and a father
who was a president of something downtown
at thirty-five. When I asked him about life
he said *You do what you do, you do it—*
Christ, you just do what you want.
My mother said *It's not that goddamn simple.*
Even at six, I felt ashamed that I was sad
when I had so much sunshine
and money and water and time.

Sometimes you open up a person
and see the soul of an empty
refrigerator. Just that old bottle

of cherries your one friend gave you
that sit there in their syrup.
I wish I were a little bit stupider,
a little bit happier, a little bit younger.

The man has almost finished eating his egg.
He tips a brown bag up to his mouth.
He tips it again. He takes a bite
of the shattered shell. Perhaps it has protein.
He marvels at the membrane that binds it
together, the same stuff that suspends
a broken windshield.

Elements

On my porch in Truro I watch the horizon
flatlining. This day, like all others,
will die. The waves lift their salty hips
to the sky. It darkens and breaks
into a sweat of stars. Each night
this dumbshow repeats. Love must live
in these elements. Even the ocean
is never satisfied, rarely calm,
no matter how many times
the sky pulls down the sun, squeezing
its color over her like the juice of a blood orange.
I hear her swell and sink on her bed of sand,
chanting *too much too much too much*.
Sometimes the sky shows off, cracks
his lightning whip till he sees her white fear.
Maybe love is the blurred and spinning line
between them, nothing more than motion.
In the bushes flowers whisper,
swing their dresses, waiting for bees
in their striped suits to suck them
and move on.
Each night the sky turns another trick
and we are no different.
Let me say tonight I am drowning.
Air blows through our mouths and moves
the water. We are shifting elements,
one more bubble, one more cloud,
waiting to be poked and broken.

Father with Cow Head

When my father calls to lecture me,
I picture him naked at the gates of heaven,
annoyed that the line's not moving faster,
noticing, for the first time—maybe because
they are all naked—the people around him.
Poked full of holes, they float right through him
and he thinks, *Where is the money?*

While my father talks, I watch my daughter draw,
winking girls in outfits from every era—
50's, a poodle skirt,
60's, patched bell bottom jeans,
90's, rollerblades
and in the background, brick walls.

There's a special report on TV.
The airplane rose like a pointed finger.
The newsman explained
that the victims had been good people
with sweet lives full of ice-skating
and second honeymoons.

The telephone drones,
Just do it, and it'll be done, Shell.

On every other channel now,
a blonde has her mouth open,
but is too scared to speak.

The wind knocks a piggy bank
off my bathroom shelf.
I can see from here

it only chipped an ear.
It's the kind you have to break
to get the money out.

My father presses all the folds
in my brain till I can't remember
what it is I'm supposed to do.
The sun stares like the hot light
in an interrogation room.

Seven years ago I had a baby
just so he would notice me.

This is all too hard.
Time for a pastoral fantasy.

If my father had the head of a cow
with the flat linoleum eyes,
nothing walking across them,
the cud, the endless chewing, chewing,
chewing up of a thing,
all of this would be easier.
A cow head,

really, would make it much easier.
I'd stick him in the yard, watch him
chew, with love I'd watch him.
Dad, his big fat head
wide as a field.

Storms swirl like stickless lollipops
across the patchwork clown suit
of our country.

I sleep well in the middle of nowhere,
and even better in the rain.
Why can't I spend
the rest of my life in the rain,
nowhere, sleeping?

Pressed against my daughter's ear,
smelling her hair, I can almost feel
the spin of the earth.

Field Trips

At the Botanic Garden we studied herbs
and spices. Ms. Lynn told us
Attila the Hun was paid off in peppercorns.
The Romans opened their gates and said
Here, don't sack us.
Attila ate Hun Steak-Au-Poivre
for weeks, till the grinder was hollow
then he sacked them.
A guide named Senta,
dressed from head to foot in orange
led us through the tropic zone.
We potted a mint plant
and got to take it home.

Did you know that real stars have numbers
and explode without anyone knowing?
Some nights I drink alone in the dark.

We studied invertebrates
at a castle in the park.
We turned over rocks
and caught them with paint brushes and spoons
careful not to crush their little spineless bodies.
They do so much for us, Ms. Esther said.
They make the soil rich,
they eat the bad guys.
A worm can divide and conquer.
The spring wind blew
the children's laughter over the hill.
On certain days I wish I were dead.

At the Time Life photo lab
we made pictures of our hands.
In the red dark, we sank shiny paper
into chemicals and saw ourselves wave.

Frank

We used to have barbecues out on the back porch with your friend Frank who I later fucked. We'd argue about politics and the way steaks should be cooked. Frank always took my side. His hobble turned me on. The sound of it. Coming from the kitchen. Expectant, defiant, optimistic, almost cocky.

But spending the night with Frank had been an eenie-meenie-miniemoe thing really. You had gone over to his house during one of my loathsome cast parties, and I'd decided I'd go home with you if you were still there, but I'd fuck Frank if you weren't. Frank had cerebral palsy. I think that's what bothered you the most. You and your philosophy of perfection. Frank looked like a gross marionette to you. God with His strings tangled had forgotten Frank. He'd never been with a woman before. It was an incredible feeling of power. I became so much bigger than life. I rode on top of him like a queen. His legs were abandoned outposts. I covered them with kisses.

The next morning was Easter. You showed up at Frank's dressed as the Easter bunny, your bike basket full of stupid chocolate eggs. You had a sarcastic fondness for all major holidays. We were in the kitchen having coffee when you knocked. We could see you through the glass but you couldn't see us. I wish I'd thought about the light. I could have hidden. Instead I sat there growing roots. Wearing my sticky silk dress from the night before. I remember blowing smoke rings although I didn't smoke so I couldn't have been, but I would have if I did. Frank hobbled to the door and let you in. His hobble sounded different in the morning. You did a self-conscious doubletake when you saw me, then rode away. Frank and I spent the rest of the day going over those two minutes.

When I went home, I discovered those frightening bunny ears you had hung on the lamp. All lit up. The ghost of the bunny cuckold. I also found the smashed clay head of John the Baptist you had brought me on our first date. Its ruined mouth leered up at me from the front walk.

A Good Green Thing

I roll a thin blue Raleigh
over the green grass of the golf course
that runs on both sides of our street.
It's a good bike, a fine bike, my father
has told me over and over again.
GET ON, he says. *NOW PUMP.*
YOU'LL FALL OVER BUT PUMP
AND PUMP BACKWARDS TO STOP.
NO, WRONG, NO, NO. WRONG. WRONG
SHELL. YOU'RE DOING IT WRONG.
Bam. The sky has swung around, grass is where
sky should be and bright bells beat music
in my ear, trying to drown out Dad.
How did I ever learn to ride? But I did.
I wobbled, but it happened. I lurched, but I moved
till it was smooth and I could leave him, a small
stick in the background,
watching, waiting for me to fall.

Hangover

I concentrate best next to piled china,
on days gray and thick as gravy.
There's something so reassuring about gloom.
It's *here,* you don't have to wait for it.
I like to sit in big cars in the rain,
dangle my feet out the window, watch the drops
dribble down my toes, smoking,
singing Herman's Hermits songs.
Nothing in my head but old relatives,
my dead mother who loved
"Mrs. Brown You've Got a Lovely Daughter,"
the nephew who took out his glass eye and rolled it around.

Yesterday I puked, then curled into the sofa
and counted the beats in my head.
Outside, work went on, the beep beep
of backing delivery trucks, drills vibrating
in the cavities of the crumbling street.
I'm turning forty-five, and I felt my liver
like a boxing glove in my side, saw the day
rise and fall patiently, like breath itself.
Where was my daughter? Printing
her spelling words, wreck and knife and glum,
or out in a playground laughing, swinging
up towards, then away from, the sun.

Here in Brooklyn

In Japan the Buddhist priest met us at the mouth of the temple with a
          cell phone to his ear.
He told us there are exactly one hundred and eight things to wish for.

A man in an undershirt washes his fish in the fire hydrant.

Certain birds can't stop flying or they'll die.

The moon winks slowly each month though it's just a trick of the light.

My father is an old man and my child is growing fast as bamboo.

My love grows too and I'm afraid it will burst apart and kill me.

I think about your heart in your chest, your legs, your arms and voice.
You take up less room in the world than a piano or a closet or a dresser
          or a hallway.

Every guy on 4th Ave. is fixing his back left tire.

Tonight we'll read, and listen to crickets and dogs and birds and
          climbing cats
here in Brooklyn.

Impunity

Living is like having an allowance
with no faces on the bills.
A lot of people tell me
they are middle-aged.
How do they know?
My mother was middle aged at twenty-nine.
At fifty-seven, she clung to my arm and said,
Let's live it up, Birdie.
We'd go to Arturo's on Houston.
She'd ask the piano player in his shoddy tux
to play "The Way You Look Tonight."
I'd lean against the waist of the piano
and while I sang, Mother watched
the drunks to make sure they were listening.
Most of them weren't,
though a few glared abstractedly
at my moving mouth.
Someday, when I'm awfully low,
when the world is cold...
When I walk past the two bedroom apartment
I should have rented twenty years ago,
Number 17 Stuyvesant Street,
I remember my mother
asking the foreign landlord,
Will my daughter be able
to come and go with impunity?
Come and go with what? he said.

Japan Dark

We wound around stairs,
stepping, turning, our hands grazing
the worn brass rail.

We went down into dark,
darker than velvet theatre curtains,
darker than black jelly beans,
darker than the eyes of insects.

We worked our way along a ridged wall
and all the tourists laughed
to toss out fear.

We were to kiss
the wall for luck,
to make us live long and well,
to make us get what we want
or even know what that might be.

A red leather jacket,
a morning in the news,
a kitchen with an island.

What does my father want
when he kisses that wall,
I wonder.

Mine is the wish of a child
blowing dandelion dust,
or picking eyelashes from daisies.

There in the dark
I want him to love me,

to store me
in a corner
of his old flabby heart.

Winding along a sticky black wall
in the sticky day
gone instantly to night,

in a temple in Japan
I want to believe
what the guide tells me.
I will have what I want.
I will have it.

I will be known
by him before it's over.
I am with him in the dark
and what we are doing
is absurd.

In the dark
we kiss stone.

John Something

He was tall, dumb and loud
and practically lived here.
He wore a suit, blue, slick and solid,
and ties with small floating things. Asterisks
or question marks. He mixed drinks,
steamed up the porch window with his talk
while I watched the pool, frozen over
like an eye, cracking like a joke.
It was winter, the light was blue-white
and made us look yellow, like passed-over
store merchandise. He was selling her
a house, which was stupid because we had
a house, but he wanted us to buy
a new one, a big one, big as his mouth.
And he always called us kid. Hey kid, how are ya, kid.
John something. And it turned dark in the room
where he laughed, dark and desperate.

A Lot of Talking in a Lot of Beds

My head has lit on this pillow before.
I've felt this muscle in another arm.
That whiskey melting in its glass
sat on a dorm room milk crate in 1978.
Do you like this music? he asks.
They always want to know
if I like their music.

Love Letter Written in the Woods

I see a low flying bee, sex plane for a flower.
A frog plays the kazoo in his throat somewhere near.
Hey Russell, Shelley here. I was composing a letter
in my head when I spotted a deer. I remember loving you,
but I don't remember why. Love has no eyes, its mouth
is a straight stitched line. Square and soft and old,
you hold it like a pillow in the dark. Before sleep
my mind pollinates a field. Russell, you need
a woman to go with your knobless door, a woman
you can stack a sack of cement in front of, to secure her.
Why do we love at all? Love is as old fashioned
as live music at the movies. But your body
is the only plot of land I own. The hill
of your carpenter's thumb, your mossy
stomach, the patch of eczema on your back
that I used to rub with cream, the hernia scar
fencing your hip since you were five,
it grew up with you. How do scars grow?
Losing your body feels to me like losing your farmland
must feel to you. One last look at the planted stand
of pines, the peas and beans, the stray cats, the shed,
even the room where we found the dead squirrel
is hard to let go of.

Mark Roblin

You were my first love, Mark Roblin. You gave me the armpit of your blue-gray cotton shirt with the little horses on it when you left for California because I liked the way it smelled. I had my first date with you. I wore my first pair of pantyhose and my first "heels," one half-inch high. We danced to "Do You Believe in Magic?" on linoleum basement tiles. Clearly you did. I remember being very impressed with your laundry chute for some reason. It had more floors to travel than ours, both attic and basement. Your mother had one bad eye. Our mothers were both drunks. They let us spend the night together because it was easier. Yours was a hot Mexican cook. I found her recipe book amid the rubble of my mother's life and thought of you, my first love. I still remember the smell of that shirt. My taste hasn't changed much.

I had a pixie haircut that summer. I was growing it out. Its elfin charm was lost on me. I didn't wash it so the dirt would drag it down. I didn't step on sidewalk cracks. I wasn't taking any chances. I felt all fluttery and stretchy inside, like I had rubber band innards every time I saw you. Our fathers were never around. Absentees they call 'em. Sounds like they stayed home from school, but it was quite the reverse. Your mother drank because she missed your dad like crazy and my mother drank because she didn't miss a thing, no matter how hard she tried.

You were some Lovin' Spoonful that night on our first date. I see the whole thing in sepia tones in my memory. I wore a white "shift" and a headband.

I remember a lot of times in the dark with you. We played hide and seek in your library and turned off all the lights. It had those pointed lead-glass windows. Your grandfather wrote "Mutiny On The Bounty." You had wonderful pajamas. Mine were sort of ripped up. Our moms would let us camp out in your library while they ate ceviche and drank martinis by our pool. They'd throw back their heads and laugh at each other's jokes, almost as if they had to gasp at the breath of fresh air of their friendship amid the suburban doldrums. I always wondered what they were laughing about.

My mom missed your mom like crazy when she left. She made friends with the next neighbors but it was never the same.

She talked about your mom one night recently. The two of us had become friends like that. I think that's what reminded her. We threw our heads back and laughed at some shared secret of life and it made her miss old Jane Roblin.

She told me she always wished your mom had gotten her eye fixed because she was so afraid she would lose it, and she was such a pretty girl. I thought that was so sweet, and somehow noble coming from someone who'd lost so much more than an eye.

Mother and Joan in the Diner

It's a dead day uptown.
Mother is dead.
Joan Crawford is dead.
There's no tension in their big florid faces.
Mother gets Joan to autograph her napkin.

"Joan, is it worth it?" Mother asks Joan.

"Worth what?" Joan says.

"Well, you know, worth it?"

"Well, what *is* it?"

"Oh, fiddle-dee-dee. *It,* all of it."

"All of what?"

"Joan," Mother changes the subject,
"can I buy you a fruit cup?"

"You *are* a fruit cup, Barbara."
They laugh. They smoke and laugh
and look at themselves in the mirror
behind their booth. Their lips are the biggest,
brightest, most frightening thing on 86th Street.
"We don't look half bad for dead women," they laugh.
"Nothing like death to give you a lift."
Every so often they rise a little
in their vinyl booth benches.
They are alike, from eyebrows—thick,
furrowed cliffs of fury—to the thin
stately ankles there on the linoleum.

Flocks of kids drift by the window,
secretaries, bums, millionaires, people
who play chess, Mother and Joan watch.
A kid misbehaves, and both
their hands come up ready to swat.
"Touché," Joan says.
They slap each other five, laugh.

The Mountain Game
for Liz

We were nine that summer, you were tan and cuter,
your pony tail auburn and longer than mine.
Our parents clinked ice and howled at the pool
while we played the game in my sweltering room.

Each time the same scenario. We slit
our fingers, rubbed our blood together.
Now I'm your older sister, you are my brother,
we're orphaned and poor. I send you
to the mountain to pick berries for dinner.
Struck by tumbling rock, you stumble, fall.

Always I hear you, always I find you,
lying there broken at the top of the stairs.
When I lift you up, you go limp as a drunk,
I carry you back to my bed to save you.
I prop pillows behind your crushed head,
douse your brow with warm wet cloths.

Although we're dirt poor we have a maid:
your brother in my mother's elbow-length
gloves that reach to his shoulders,
strands of pearls, her slip, a veiled hat,
lipstick smeared on his four year old face.
He stands on hand with a bowl of water.

I take your temperature with a straw
and send our maid off for strong medicine.

The rule is you keep your eyes closed
while I pull off your top, your shorts,
wrap you in towels, place your head in my lap,
bend down till our ponytails are one golden rope,

kiss your forehead, your temples, your ears,
your throat, your flat chest, death is so close
I can taste it on your short breaths—

as I hear our maid trip on his slip
up the stairs, bearing the cure
the real maid has helped him prepare.
I spoon magic broth into your mouth,
your eyelids flutter open.

Big sister, I'm sorry about the berries.
You're alive, little brother, that's all that matters.

We wriggle into damp swim suits,
run down the mountain stairs,
jump into the shallow end,
splashing the bleary adults.

It was strange to see you in L.A., aging
and gray, your skin a sun-dried brown,
in a gay trailer park on the Pacific Palisades,
your brother, a decorator, a few trailers away.

You watch home movies of that summer
over and over, you think about me constantly,
you said. I think about you when I'm with
a man, once again trying to abandon myself—
I never can—the way I did when we played orphan—

Here's what's true, Liz—
When we were nine, I loved your body
in my bed completely, maybe
the same way you could still love mine.

(Victoria's Secrets Are) My Sister's Secrets

Her man calls her from a sky phone, from his car phone and they talk dirty. She meets him by the pool at the Bel Air Hotel in L.A. He buys her dinner and Shirley Temple drinks. After his credit card has been squeezed into the restaurant's small metal bed, she gives it all to him. Her body, her confidences.

He is an architect and she is impressed with his credentials. She tells me his skin feels loose and dry like leather. Like a wallet, I am thinking. It is forty-five-year-old skin. I have never felt this. It is successful skin. It is skin with a four bedroom house, skin from Yale, skin of a married man. A man she can never call. A man whose calls she has to wait for. She can't call him at the office because he fucks his secretary too.

But she is happy for the weekends she gets, weekends she could afford to buy for herself fifty times over. She doesn't do it for the money. She hopes his worth will rub off on her while they go at it. While their sweat mingles, some of his valuable salt will sink into her raw white skin and stay there. She's happy to wear her white garter belt with the matching stockings, her perfume, her gold studs. She is like a glossy photo in a brochure. Her whispered intimacies are like captions or slogans. She is like Vanna White on the Wheel of Fortune. Standing to the side of the game, all dressed up and clapping. He is a daddy and a brother and a lover all in one, and maybe a teacher and a boss too.

As she passes the gilt mirrors in the Bel Air lobby, she is not like me. Not falling for men with sad, musty smelling skin, skin full of memory, that can't be replaced if you lose it. As she passes those mirrors she is our mother, a younger version of our mother. The Dorian Gray portrait of our mother, whose laughter always cascades down some exhaust pipe into a courtyard filled with strangers.

The Only Star You Can See from New York

Summer in April, early in this strange
new century, a restaurant in Williamsburg,
we sat at an outside table, and smoked
a cigarette. Venus winked in the hot sky
over a line of hung laundry, a necklace
of blue and green T-shirts, white boxer shorts,
a tiny training bra dangling in the center like a jewel.

It was the best cigarette I ever smoked,
the reason, in fact, that people smoke—
a perfect pause between courses—after
the octopus, before the artichoke ravioli,
after meeting, talking,
before the sweet surprise of sleeping
with someone who could be my son.
Then, like a change of scene in a play,
a woman from a window stage right
reeled the fresh clothes in.

Later, in bed, his eyes safely closed, I looked at him,
curled in his S of sleep, long neck, burst of black hair
over white white skin, an awkward, adolescent cat
who hasn't grown into his ears or arms or legs quite yet.
I lost my virginity the year Sam was born, I heard
*Hey Jude, don't make it bad…*walked into the woods to a cave
while the tenth graders swayed on the dance floor like bears.
Sam collects vintage shirts. Under this worn skin
my heart beats backwards.

Pants

The city is full of pants. I am a woman buying pants and when I find them I will have pants, I will have a past and a future and I will shop for a top. My dad invested in futures *YOU'RE GONNA RUN OUT, SHELL* which I guess are fortunes, but are not found in cookies. It's all very complicated. *ONE OF THESE DAYS YOU'RE GOING TO HAVE TO WORK.* The rules of this store are the new rules of life. Age/Size 42, a perfect fit, my father's hand on my back as I walk the aisles. *Ma'am, do you need any help?* When my father dies I will have vision. Till then walls drip and whisper around me. *We'll be closing in five minutes.* I will find one perfect thing, then another till I build a life. *Ma'am, both sizes look great on you. Maybe you should take both.* Tight or loose? *SHELL, LISTEN.* Ten or Twelve? *YOU'RE GOING TO* Which is right? *RUN OUT OF MONEY* I try on the same pants in different sizes *AT A VERY AWKWARD* back and forth *AGE.* If I were a better person I could solve this. There has to be an answer right here *YOU'VE BEEN FUCKING AROUND* in these pants. *FOR TWENTY GODDAMN YEARS* Somebody switched pairs *AND ONE OF THESE DAYS* when I wasn't looking, *YOU'RE GOING TO HAVE TO* the pants seem different now, they're grabbing me *WORK* in the crotch, *SHELL, FACE IT* clinging to my legs. *Do you want me to hold the pants for you?* The pants are holding me, *STOP FUCKING AROUND.* The mirror is tricky, flat, *Ma'am, you'll have to make up your mind, we're closing.* Someone's on the floor now, pulling at my pant leg. *Ma'am, are you all right in there?* The pants are twisting like vines, I beat at them with my shoe. *Is there anything I can do, ma'am?* I don't know, I don't think so.

Perimenopausal Pelvic Sonogram

In the opening scene
of this short bleak documentary
my ovaries roll like tumbleweeds
down an ill-lit narrowing highway.

A metal bus swerves and turns inside me,
taking pictures like a pack of tourists.

My IUD blinks bright, a neon sign
advertising an all night bar,
GIRLS GIRLS GIRLS
the only place open
in this broken-down ghost town.

The doctor drives by boarded-up buildings,
full of rooms once chandelier-grand
where girls kicked their legs high
on polished dance floors.

Here on the metal table
in my half-open paper robe
with a microphone-curling-iron-dildo-
shaped thing shoved up my cunt
I hear that Karen Carpenter song
"On Top of the World."

I remember riding the Central Park
carousel with my soon-to-be ex-
husband. The big-veined carny man
who pulled the lever to make the horses
speed looked just like him.
The organ pipes wheezed out
loud cheery Karen Carpenter songs—

I'm looking down on creation...
and I pictured her disappearing
inside her all-American clothes,
her career the only remaining flesh on her.

Why do women want to disappear?

Your lining looks good,
no fibroids, the doctor says.
He points to a line, faint as a watermark.
The lining of my leather coat
has shredded where my ass rubs.

I thought of the secretive way
I folded it around itself
when I took off my clothes.

The doctor turns off the machine.
On the screen now is a tornado
my ovaries are swept up into like lawn chairs.

Pie

I bought a crust at the all night Sloan's
and filled it up with apples,
cinnamon, butter and sugar,
slapped another crust upside down on top,
scored it so the apples would bubble out,
and I cooked it and felt better.
I got the recipe from my therapist
who used to feed me in the days when I was so distracted
I couldn't sleep or eat. I remember long walks
and long spiraling conversations, and the small
comfort of hugging my husband's back.
I don't think I've ever had a bad time eating pie.
When I was a kid Mother picked rhubarb
from our fence and boiled it, Grandma made key lime
and I never understood what that key meant,
and Barbara, my therapist, made apple pie
and sometimes I think she threw in nuts
for crunch and it was just what I needed,
late at night, starved from my inheritance.

Quit It

I'm outside, it's not raining,
the meal is good, I have a child
and both my breasts, half my
trust fund, a good quarter
of my life. I have to give up
some things. Clank—like plates
taken away—I'll never be
a young success, I won't have
another childhood, I may never find
love. He's whining. He's everyone
I've fucked. Piled horizontally my men would
reach up a couple of stories.
Head-to-toe vertically maybe
twenty-five floors. He's Yertle
the turtle at the top of the stack,
I'm just a plain turtle at the bottom named Mack.
Pardon, your majesty.
Later he will scream at me
as if he's throwing up. I will
rub his neck till it's over, watch him
walk out the door for the last time
again. The carpet will look
particularly red. They say
the Paris plane flew for seconds
without a cockpit, passengers watched
the O of sky in front of them,
held aloft by nothing.
There's a time before dark
when everything is ringed in light
as if in quotes and the air
is the breath of God. This Sunday
I had a sudden need to go
to church. The gruesome Jesus,

his loincloth slipping as he bleeds,
is the sexiest thing I've ever seen.
I was in Chatham when the plane crashed,
riding my bike past rambling roses
and a vegetable stand where once a week
the sign said, "Sorry. Closed. Growing today."
When the gynecologist poked at my breasts
I thought about my insurance.
Pure and perfect. It covers nothing.
Are you finished, Ma'am?
He takes away another plate. Life.
A kind of compression, curdled cream.
Dessert? I don't want it. Just deserts,
I want those. Next Sunday
from my bed I'll hear plates
being stacked in the restaurant kitchen
below me, try to work them
into a masturbation fantasy.
When I was in sixth grade
I tortured a girl named Pamela Chertak.
She's dead now for other
reasons. She was sick and small
and as if that wasn't enough, she had warts
all over her twisted hands. Looking at her
was like wiggling a loose tooth.
I played what I called the Quit It game.
I poked and poked and pinched
her pink pig skin till she squealed
Quit it, which always took
longer than it should have. It made me
angry that she wouldn't stop me.
The last time he was in my bed
he flipped me over, pushed me down.

I want to take you from behind,
he snarled. He wouldn't kiss me till I cried.
Then he called me Cupcake.
I wish I could say I was crying
for those people dying in the plane
but I'm not, I want my mother. It's pathetic
to envy people who have burned to death
like marshmallows, but I do.
Like a crazy person, I hold
a lemon, a wadded up tissue, a leaky pen,
as if the answer is in their connection.
I spray lemon in my eyes, wipe the tears
with tissue, try to get it all down
while I still sting.

Rabbit's Foot

You are the rabbit's foot tucked in my pocket.
I stroke you when I'm nervous, unsure, upset.
You keep my counsel, soft and silent.
A chain hangs from the shiny top
that hides the place where they lopped you off,
and from the chain, a key.
In dreams, on a bed of fresh wet grass,
reattached, your body hops whole to me.
You are all your parts combined and each
part individually: lost and found foot,
link, opener of the locked,
a way in, a way out.
Talisman of animal pain,
chained lameness, you are my luck.

Ready for Winter

Leaning over the laundry machines
in the basement of the house where we stayed
that first year of Summer Stock, I told you
the story that made people hate me or want me
immediately. How I grew up rich, raised
by a drunk mother who came at me with a knife—
I'd told it so much, it didn't even feel true.
You hung up our costumes and listened.
You never talked and I liked that.
That night in the hall I kissed you for hours.
I don't remember you, just me, just what I did.

The next day someone gave me a tiny flower,
said it was from you. That one tiny wilted flower,
picked, probably, from the parking lot.

After you moved out, I found the wall
of boxes wedged tight as puzzle pieces
in the closet we called yours.
Everything I was through with,
carefully labeled and saved.
An almost empty pack of breast pads,
cracked rubber nipples in yellowing bottles,
the lucite frame with the sample
picture of a couple still in it.
I see you each weekend walk away with our child.

The Retreat

Look at nuns long enough
shower with nuns
eat and shit and sit in the sun with nuns
look at them
how they chew
humble and heavy and satisfied with food
and the one man they share like Mormons.
They walk hand in hand
to the bowl of water
and splash, shedding years
till I see the girl in them from before they took the vows.
One nun with a crooked back
one with a nose too big
one with a bum leg
one with a face like a wrinkled potato
they come in pairs to the water, girls again.
We ride the old bikes off the grounds
up the hill and back
wade and swim in the algae-green water
slowly and silently
pray to him.

Russell's Dream

I was in this big dairy barn, but it was weird, I have to say.

Why was it weird, Russell?

I was milking women instead of cows
and I didn't know if I was supposed to herd them downstairs
or let them come on their own.

What did they look like?

That wasn't really the dynamic.

What were they wearing?

Panties, I think, and these long bra things that looked sort of medieval.

Bustiers?

Is that what they're called?

Did you have to coax their tits out of their outfits?

They sort of popped out.

Did it turn you on?

Kind of, but I was worried about my job.
I had to get the buckets lined up just right
or the milk sprayed out over the side.
It was complicated.

Were they fat?

Who?

Who do you think? The cowgirls, Russell.

No, not really. Why?

Were they good looking?

What do you mean?

What do you think I mean?

I guess so, but that really wasn't the dynamic.

Russell's Lament

He told me he will lose his childhood land.
"This will sound stupid," he said,
"but I won't be able to drive a tractor
over fields anymore, and that's always
been an option."

Walking his bike through Boerum Hill
to the house he bought four years ago,
where nothing is renovated except
the door. Bricks, wood, wires
sit useless, like his farm in Iowa
where corn once counted for something.

He adjusted the volume on his ten cent
stereo, lit the tall candle I gave him
for Christmas, asked if I wanted
water, and I lay there with my legs
crossed, my arms crossed over my head,
wearing nothing but a lipstick
we would make disappear.

Scattered Rain in Iowa

Dean does something complicated
in a bathroom behind the kitchen,
while his adopted parents
tell us town history.
The watercolor over the sofa,
that's her grandfather, a hunter,
the first man to poke his blind gun
into the caves that have made
Maquoketa a tourist town.
She did not get lucky with this boy.
Her face is gray and creased
like the sheets on the bed
where he lives out his sentence,
dominated by the noun, also adjective,
which sounds like it applies
to reptiles or mollusks or slugs
or sad square buildings
where men march to death in place.
Quadriplegic.

The van ramp rumbles up.
We drive past corn rows,
the hairdo in its original form.
The clouds are popcorn-shaped
as if the crops have transmogrified
here in God's country.
At the quarry we let him down,
a slow bug on a silver leaf.
He rolls to the water,
baits his hook, casts and waits,
dragonflies mate in mid-air
over his head.

Dean in a wheelchair
without anything
below the neck
but a hidden cave,
dark and dripping.
Fishing from the wheelchair,
casting with his special rod
he bought from TV,

he can push it with one thumb.
Pepsi in the stand,
in the hot sun in his safari hat.

What would this be like?
Me without money.
Me without lovers,
without my mother,
me without my daughter,
without my father,
without a husband.

Dean flying through the window
of a jackknifing horse truck,
Dean in the ditch, his legs
like dropped grocery bags.

Me without mutual funds,
me without stocks and bonds,
without time.

Dean's time spilling from him
like reams of serrated print-out,

TV, sleep, the full, then empty, catheter—
a pocket to store one Pepsi.

When I make my million, Dean says, sipping it,
I'm gonna have a hydro-chair I can swim in,
jet propelled.

Do they make those? I ask.

I'm gonna float through this quarry
catching fish with my bare hands.
I'll live on that hill there,
and look down here at my stocked pond
and I won't need to ride in a van.
I'll hire a pretty nurse to push me.
I'll fish everyday. Every single blessed day. I will.

Green fields rustle
like the drum roll of cash at an ATM.
In Iowa, you can see rain fall on your neighbor
while the sun still shines on you.
I rip the dollar in my pocket
and toss it in the water, a wish.
God, one side says.
Trust, says the other.

Serengeti Plain

A man walking with a stick at the edge
of the road, tossed up and over a car
that didn't even break its speed, dead in the ditch
when we zoomed from the airport to Nairobi—
Welcome to Africa: In a tin can car
I thought how easy—one spin of the wheel
and I wouldn't have to know how it all turned out.
Seeing a man thrown many feet, hearing
the little plop of his life ending, did nothing
to increase my sense of life's importance.
One quick meal for a passing carnivore.
But the wild animals didn't roam this strip
of exotica, just other toy cars like ours,
driven by very black men in white suits
and gloves with complicated names
full of n's and o's.

Later, on the plain, we saw two lions fuck.
It took three hours of roaring foreplay then was
over in ten seconds, lasting only slightly longer
than the accident. We followed a pack
of wild dogs in our zebra-striped vans
and jeeps belonging to photographers
who'd waited days for the dogs to move.
Asleep under the only clump of trees
for miles, the leader dog woke up, appeared
to bite the neck of one of his ugly patchy brothers,
a show of trust, our guide said, part of the ritual.
One bit the next, that one the next and so on
until all throats had been exposed, threatened, spared.
Then the leader lifted his head to sniff the evening air.

On an invisible signal the dogs took off
in formation, a killing machine, precise as birds,
deadly they ran and swerved to invisible instructions,
took down a wildebeest, a baby, one unlucky baby
who lagged behind. They didn't knock him down
initially, but eviscerated him where he stood,
crowding around his belly like men at a bar.
The sun had sunk the whole Serengeti
blood shot, then purple, then an indefinable
mix of colors that ended up as gray.
My stepmother pouted, slumped
in the back of the van.
Jeez, this is fantastic, my father said, *look at it, Shell,
nature, it's wild.* My stepmother said, *I know it's nature
but I don't have to look at it.* You couldn't see much
except shadows. The noise was the shocking part.
A quiet satisfied crunching in the darkening night.

Seven and Six

Saturday in childhood. Above me,
around me, adults are in adulthood.
I am seven, a slanted number,
and my brother is six.
The owner of the station cigar shop,
the man with the donut nose,
gives me a box to keep.
I open and close its lid on the El train,
thinking of all the troll clothes I will store in it,
flat felt strips with two holes
for the straight plastic arms.
The train screeches and skids towards
Chicago, past those lives I see close-up
for a second, and expand into movies.
The hot slow tenements lean
toward us, their windows whisper
unambitious secrets. Graying
underpants hang like faces on the line.
Socks and bras dangle like commas.
My brother and I both ride
this train, our bent knees look the same,
but someday he'll teach his son to fold a flag,
he'll become a flag folder.

On this Saturday in childhood
we're riding to my father's office
where there's a big computer
that takes up a whole room.
We pass other fathers
sitting on porches, we intersect
with them like thread through
cloth, a needle pierced then
pulled, moving to make something
you can hold. Birds blow backwards
across the tracks, trash flies like birds,
and we ride like grown-ups, downtown.

Seymour

Icy snow attacks the square where white
statues, a couple, stand, in their element
now, everything around them turning
white, the wind so strong it sounds like
someone shaking out wet sheets.
In the pet shop window, puppies
huddle on their bed of shredded
documents. Four days since my last
cat, Seymour, died. His ashes will
arrive today in what the crematory calls
an attractive—or is it decorative?—tin.
He was born the year I played Jeannie
in *Hair*, I was the oldest in that Age
of Aquarius cast, thirty-four, I loved
to prance naked offstage past the
orchestra boys. I wish I had some
Lincoln Logs. I'd build a cabin and
shrink my ego to fit into it. Branches
swing back now, shattering spring
leaves. The neon SmoKING sign
with its royal pipe winks next to
the liquor store run by Mr. Wang,
the wine expert, whom I used to
distract with quality questions and
food questions so he wouldn't notice
the vast volume. *Will this go with salmon?*
I'd ask when what I meant was
Will this go with madness and despair?

Sidecar

I walked to the end of the driveway
turned left, kicked shells all the way around
the bend till I couldn't see, couldn't hear
her calling to the gardener. I'd hear the mower
stop and sigh, click like a clucking tongue
while he banged her in his straw gardener's hat,
his neck hard and coarse as rope. I walked
all the way to the next stop, waited
for the yellow bus where no one
knew my mother. I took comfort
in my oversized cotton jacket,
a cool cloud around my bony body.
But I could hear her shriek a mile away.
Sometimes the furniture man, Ed True
with the munchkin voice, fucked Mom too.
The milkman who brought the bone-
shaped dog biscuits she snacked on
with liquor. And like the sidecar
on a motorcycle I had my boys,
big boys with Adam's apples the size of super balls
who'd been in the eighth grade four times
and drank and drove and broke and entered.
I rode another bus, to pass cigarettes to them
through small windows in the jail cell door.
I hardly remember Steve Hornikel's face
but I see the sooty square window
I held his hand through.

Silhouettes

If my parents had been poor,
if they'd stayed in Hyde Park
in the apartment on the top floor
with the turrets, sun in the morning
streaming in like hope,
the blue at night still just blue, me
in the hall, cooing, sleeping
while they played cards and thick LPs
would they have made it?

Summer, fireworks on the roof,
that old green blanket they had to throw away
after the storm got it.
Winter, maps of bare trees on the ceiling,
their lives wandered like rivers then
and all they had to do was swim.
Meat smelled good simmering
in that small warm apartment.

Two windows on a block,
two squares of light,
two people just beginning.
The day my father drove me down
we sat in the Cadillac out in front
of the now grown over vacant lot.
That's where it was, he said.
It was there, right there.

Snow Day

Snow is a leveler. Tomorrow, it says,
all this will be remembered, the lost
shoe, lost check, but today is pure
and sparkling, a celebration of firsts.

Six and sinking hip deep into it, building
a fort with retarded Tommy Watson,
our breath businesslike while we dug the walls,
workers, not one smarter than the other,
snowpackers and secret tunnel makers.

It stuck to branches and turned the trees
into lacy communion dresses. We ate it,
risking radioactivity, scary as Red China
and Russia, tiny bits of bombs
that might explode inside us later, or make us
shine green as Gatorade.

Narrowing paths and dogs dancing
circles in it, and the scrape of shovels
across the street, the Scandinavian sisters
in their knitted hats, maybe lesbians

and the man who gave out dimes on Halloween
hired a boy we didn't know to shovel his snow.
We shoveled ours into mountains on the sides,
my dropped glove a soggy leaf we'd find in spring.

*   *   *

Today although it's still winter,
it rained, dark and dirty.
All the double parked trucks splashed
with the back slap of the road, people
moving in and out of places gripping
plastic bags, wrestling umbrellas
with broken metal bones.

Mike and I walked down the street
under the biggest umbrella, big as a picnic
umbrella, arm in arm we strutted, everyone
parted and stared. In the sky a boom
then fast vision of a ladder of light,
the majesty of weather.

My great grandfather was struck by lightning
collapsing a patio umbrella, in a field
in Kentucky. Weather dictates,
then abruptly changes. Lately,
do you feel it weakening?

There's a hole in the ceiling,
a boiler in the basement groaning,
radiators knocking. *Come in,*
we would say if we were home.
Earth is a hotel, rain is a lazy maid.

We are made of water and when we die
we'll see again that tunnel of snow
we worked so hard to build
as children. It's the white light
the ones who travel halfway, then
come back, describe.

Until then, let's hide in our rebel den,
pull out the slippers, the books, the stack
of ready wood, and burn this life
into ourselves like a brand.

Somewhere, My Love

I waited in the anteroom of the small church
in Maine where Bryan's parents married, no heat,
no electricity. One of the aunts pounded out
"Somewhere My Love" on the untuned organ.

Outside the window, I saw the small plot
of headstones, my intended's dead relatives.
Funny word, intended. Do we do what we intend?
I never picked this music for my entrance.

Earlier at the rehearsal my father directed,
Before you walk to the altar, stand a second,
Shell, so everyone can see the dress. He blocked
the scene, the dramatic pause, in his suit.

The right side of the audience
wore overalls over naked chests,
many were missing teeth. I took stage
in my $3400 Chinese lace wedding dress,
they caught their collective country breath.

Repeat after me, the minister began
in his Bar Harbor inflection—*Braayun*—
I repeated the name exactly how he said it.
(I am the only person I know
who got a laugh on the wedding vow.)

My love was somewhere, but not at that altar.
My love that day was for my father,
more out of place than I was, as he watched me stop
to show off that classy gown he'd bought,
before I crossed to Bryan and lied,
Till death do us part.

20 years ago on Halloween, we were costumed
as bride and groom. I remember that room,
that song, the rightness and wrongness of it.

Spinners

Frank took me to dinner, drank a pink drink
with a cherry. Bourbon Manhattan. Talked
about spinners, which I learned are young girls
you can twirl around on your dick. The boundaries
have collapsed and there's a man next to my left ear.
He's whispering *Maybe not.* I'm too fast. I can't think
in the dark. My life is a tangled up underwear drawer,
each pair a different encounter.

What makes me drink too much? When will I die?
Before my brother? After my father? What order
will we line up in? Tallest first or last? Best first or last?

Behind the scroll of sky a big mouth blows cold and it snows.
The leaves are yellow today. Somewhere in a yard
in the suburbs a man is raking. A bike spins its wheel
on a driveway. A car motor clicks in the cold
afternoon. A door creaks shut. A life continues
blind, feeling its way forward
with its white stick of days.

There's a picture of me kissing my brother's
cheek on a sofa that is blue and square.
It's 1962 and my ears are big. I'm smarter
than I will be later, today, looking at the picture
on a sofa with candle wax spilled on the pillows
from a party and it smells of smoke
from the stranger I kissed last night.

When my eyes were closed he was everything good,
every Christmas morning, but now it's a gray Saturday
afternoon, the leaves are shaking, my hand shakes
from a hangover and the picture shakes in it.
The things my father told me are true.
There are no chances once you make a mistake.
His cheeks are fat and young. Maybe I will rip this picture up now.

Talking to God

Walking along the Hudson towards Battery
Park, battered still after 9/11, I'm listening
to a set of tapes called *Conversations*
with God. This angry guy wrote God a ranting
letter, then channeled the answer.
Ed Asner takes turns with Ellen Burstyn
playing God, who is not just one controlling
uber-man, but every person, every part
of every smidgen of every little thing
except religion. The angry guy asked
many questions, but they simmer down
to this: *How do you choose the head*
on which the falling brick will land?
Now, after all this build-up, here it is,
God's answer, here it is, God's plan:
Here it is—God's answer was Everything Is.
The sky along the river is, but is
also always becoming. Gray is
never consistent, even when
a depressed person stares at rain.
Ron says he won't run along the river
anymore, he doesn't feel worthy,
so he runs on the Bowery.
The decaying stumps of old docks
rise from the water like grave markers
in a potter's field. I round the Japanese
bridge past the Finance Center's palm
tree court, is that back again or gone?
So much has changed I forget what was
there before, even those two buildings
biting into heaven like bonded teeth.
It's possible to feel lost limbs' ghost pain,
they say. It's so big, even one minute

along the Hudson, this one short strip
from Christopher Street, patron saint
of travelers, to the bottom of Battery Park.
I could pace it for a lifetime, die
before I clearly see it, die before
I figure out the point.

Thirteen

You bent over me in the doorway
of Three Lives Books, all elbows,
as if caught in a country song.
Your coat flapped behind you.
If this were your poem, a bum would piss
now in just the right corner.

I had a child still in diapers.
Even then, your teeth were gravestones,
smoking teenagers swapping stories
on your tongue.
That's why you kissed so well.

When I stood naked in your rooming house
I didn't know you had AIDS,
I just knew you were dangerous.
I could this minute trace the fishbone
scar where they replaced
your stomach with a rubber bag.

"Tell my future," you whispered to the sky
in your chapbook "Terminal Hotel."
You announced at dinner
that you'd tried to kill yourself
twelve times. Now, *that's* failure,
my husband said later, impressed.

Vacation House, August 1997

The trees are hung with salty bathing suits.
Deck chairs creak and groan and wait.
The ocean snores, raises white eyebrows,
collapses on itself. I wonder if the hearts
of birds hum as fast as electric razors.
Stooped now, his head down, he grunts past.
Can I bring you something, Dad?
He swats the air where my question buzzes.
A plastic bag hugs, then slaps the railing.
What's this goddamn thing?
A sink, a back porch, a screen door,
a life, how could we miss it?

Yaddo

I'm disgusted by my nicotine nookie fingers,
their grope-at-the-beach sea urchin smell.
How did your work go today? they'll ask at dinner.
Oh I just beat off. No one would admit that,
but a fool or an exhibitionist, or both.
I wish I were a bat. I'd hang upside down
in a corner and smile. When people ask
what I do for a living, I'd say, *I'm a bat.*
That would cover everything.
Verb. Noun. Crouched in a doorframe,
wide and zooming. It's what I do, it's who
I am. Being a bat is my job. A masterbat. Aha!
If there's a belfry, I'll be in it. I'll ring
my bell any which way I want. Clip close
to the worm-infested planets of human heads
and whisper radar secrets. *I'm on a whole
different wavelength from these people,* I'll be thinking.
No one can quite classify me. Midget cat,
airborne rat, furred bird with monkey hands.
I'll terrorize long-haired pretty women.
Their fright will get me off.
At parties I'll say *I'm a bat* and see how men react.
I used a line when I dropped out of college
that got me a lot of attention.
What do you do?
Nothing, I'd say, *and it's incredibly hard because I'm so smart.*
Then I did my hard nothing, and in the morning
shower, I watched the film run down, tracking problems
from the drinking, and once the clap—why do they call it
the clap, like that clapper that turns lights on or off?
Gonorrhea sounds like the name
of one of Lear's wicked daughters.
Crazy, he found them all dear.

I met a deer in the woods the other day.
I was wearing my deer skin hat, and this deer
let me get very close. I watched it sink its knifed neck
to the ground and chew. It even wagged its tail
like that seeing-eye dog who struts through town
past unemployed Dalmatians—an important
dog, a dog with a job. *What do you do?*
other dogs might ask him. Most dogs have to answer
Pee and shit and lick my balls, but this dog can reply,
I went to school, received my degree in seeing-eye.
That's certainly more than I can say.

You Didn't Last
for Mother

You didn't last as long as my cat.

You didn't last as long as your Woolworth's rhododendron.

You didn't last as long as my tortoise

or the woman in the 103rd Street subway station
with bags on her feet and the distended stomach
who hasn't changed her clothes in 8 years.

You didn't last as long as my paint job

or my wallpaper

or the silk flowers I gave you

or the ashtray shaped like a fan you gave me

or my burglar bars

or my neighbors

or my marriage

or my brother's marriage

or my sister's divorce.

You didn't last as long as the tube of Revlon peach lipstick you gave me

or your glycerin soap I took

or the table you bought for me in New Orleans

that this typewriter is sitting on.

You didn't last as long as I expected you to.

You didn't last as long as my Christmas tree stand.
Most of the bulbs have survived, outlived you too.
You didn't last as long as your coffeemaker.

You didn't last as long as the Polaroid I took of you
in front of the "OUT" door of a summer theatre kitchen.

You didn't last as long as your stationery with the big lips on it.

You didn't last as long as your white beret which is still white
incidentally.

You didn't last as long as the potholders shaped like leaves you gave me

or your TV tray

or your electric toothbrush

or the last tube of toothpaste you bought

or your eyeliner pencil

or your supply of ice cubes

or your jewelry,
but we knew that would outlive you.

You didn't last as long as you didn't last as long you didn't last as you
didn't last you didn't you.

About NYQ Books™

NYQ Books™ was established in 2009 as an imprint of The New York Quarterly Foundation, Inc. Its mission is to augment the *New York Quarterly* poetry magazine by providing an additional venue for poets already published in the magazine. A lifelong dream of NYQ's founding editor, William Packard, NYQ Books™ has been made possible by both growing foundation support and new technology that was not available during William Packard's lifetime. We are proud to present these books to you and hope that you will continue to support The New York Quarterly Foundation, Inc. and our poets and that you will enjoy these other titles from NYQ Books™:

Barbara Blatner	*The Still Position*
Amanda J. Bradley	*Hints and Allegations*
rd coleman	*beach tracks*
Joanna Crispi	*Soldier in the Grass*
Ira Joe Fisher	*Songs from an Earlier Century*
Sanford Fraser	*Tourist*
Tony Gloeggler	*The Last Lie*
Ted Jonathan	*Bones & Jokes*
Richard Kostelanetz	*Recircuits*
Iris Lee	*Urban Bird Life*
Kevin Pilkington	*In the Eyes of a Dog*
Jim Reese	*ghost on 3rd*
F. D. Reeve	*The Puzzle Master and Other Poems*
Jackie Sheeler	*Earthquake Came to Harlem*
Jayne Lyn Stahl	*Riding with Destiny*
Norman Stock	*Pickled Dreams Naked*
Tim Suermondt	*Just Beautiful*
Douglas Treem	*Everything so Seriously*
Oren Wagner	*Voluptuous Gloom*
Joe Weil	*The Plumber's Apprentice*
Pui Ying Wong	*Yellow Plum Season*
Fred Yannantuono	*A Boilermaker for the Lady*
Grace Zabriskie	*Poems*

Please visit our website for these and other titles:

www.nyqbooks.org

www.ingramcontent.com/pod-product-compliance
Lightning Source LLC
LaVergne TN
LVHW011429080426
835512LV00005B/345